Proverbs, Promises, and Principles

Vern McLellan

HARVEST HOUSE PUBLISHERS
Eugene, Oregon 97402

PROVERBS, PROMISES & PRINCIPLES

Copyright © 1986 by Harvest House Publishers
Eugene, Oregon 97402

ISBN 0-89081-460-0

Printed in the United States of America.

Proverb

He who lives without principle never draws much interest.

Promise

The selfish man quarrels against every sound principle of conduct by demanding his own way (Proverbs 18:1 TLB).

Principle

He who would be great must be fervent in his prayers, fearless in his principles, firm in his purposes, and faithful in his promises.

Proverb

He who cries over spilt milk should condense it.

Promise

...I am still not all I should be but I am bringing all my energies to bear on this one thing: Forgetting the past and looking forward to what lies ahead, I strain to reach the end of the race and receive the prize for which God is calling us up to heaven because of what Christ Jesus did for us (Philippians 3:13 TLB).

Principle

When you can think of yesterday without regret and tomorrow without fear, you are near real contentment.

Proverb

He who looks down on his neighbors is usually living on a bluff.

Promise

Wisdom and good judgment live together, for wisdom knows where to discover knowledge and understanding. If anyone respects and fears God, he will hate evil. For wisdom hates pride, arrogance, corruption and deceit of every kind (Proverbs 8:12,13 TLB).

Principle

The proud man counts his newspaper clippings—the humble man his blessings—Bishop Fulton J. Sheen.

Proverb

He stands best who kneels most.

Promise

One day Jesus told his disciples a story to
illustrate their need for constant prayer and
to show them that they must keep praying
until the answer comes (Luke 18:1 TLB).

Principle

If your knees are knocking, kneel on them.
The quickest way to get back on your feet is
to get down on your knees.

Proverb

He who pats himself on the back may dislocate his shoulder.

Promise

To quarrel with a neighbor is foolish; a man with good sense holds his tongue. Pride ends in a fall, while humility brings honor (Proverbs 11:12; 29:23 TLB).

Principle

Conceit is the most incurable disease that is known to the human soul. Great braggers are small doers.

Proverb

He who tells you he is boss at his house
will also lie about other things.

Promise

A truthful witness does not deceive, but a
false witness pours out lies (Proverbs 14:5
NIV).

Principle

A lie can go around the world while truth is
getting its boots on.

Proverb

He who has been sick and thinks he is well
is in grave danger.

Promise

The wise man looks ahead. The fool
attempts to fool himself and won't face facts
(Proverbs 14:8 TLB).

Principle

Self-deception is a short blanket—if you pull
it over your face, you expose your feet.

Proverb

He who has a head of wax must not walk in
the sun.

Promise

A wise man is cautious and avoids danger; a
fool plunges ahead with great confidence
(Proverbs 14:16 TLB).

Principle

Common sense is the sixth sense (though
not as common as it used to be), given to us
by God to keep the other five from making
fools of themselves—and us.

Proverb

He who works diligently in the monogram
business will achieve *initial* success.

Promise

If you love sleep, you will end in poverty.
Stay awake, work hard, and there will be
plenty to eat! (Proverbs 20:13 TLB).

Principle

Nature gave me two ends—one to sit on and
one to think with. Man's success or failure
is dependent on the one he uses most.

Proverb

He who cannot mind his own business
should not be trusted with the king's.

Promise

It is better to trust the Lord than to put
confidence in men. It is better to take refuge
in him than in the mightiest king! (Psalm
118:8,9 TLB).

Principle

Business know-how is when a fellow knows
his business and what's none of his
business.

Proverb

He who wants eggs must endure cackling hens.

Promise

Knowing that the testing of your faith produces endurance. And let endurance have its perfect result, that you may be perfect and complete, lacking in nothing (James 1:3,4 NAS).

Principle

The bird that flutters least is longest on the wing—William Cowper.

Proverb

He who is faultless is lifeless.

Promise

Admit your faults to one another and pray
for each other so that you may be healed.
The earnest prayer of a righteous man has
great power and wonderful results (James
5:16 TLB).

Principle

A fault which humbles a man is of more
value to him than a good action which puffs
him up.

Proverb

He who plants a tree plants for posterity.

Promise

The wise man saves for the future, but the foolish man spends whatever he gets (Proverbs 21:20 TLB).

Principle

I have known personal disappointments and despair. But always the thought of tomorrow has buoyed me up. I have looked to the future all my life. I still do. I still believe that with courage and intelligence we can make the future bright with fulfillment— Bernard M. Baruch.

Proverb

He who asks faintly begs a denial.

Promise

And so it is with prayer—keep on asking
and you will keep on getting; keep on
looking and you will keep on finding; knock
and the door will be opened. Everyone who
asks, receives; all who seek, find; and the
door is opened to everyone who knocks
(Luke 11:9,10 TLB).

Principle

Pray hardest when it is hardest to pray.
Prayer is a powerful thing, for God has
bound and tied Himself thereto—Martin
Luther.

Proverb

He who stumbles twice over the same stone deserves to break his shins.

Promise

The steps of good men are directed by the Lord. He delights in each step they take. If they fall it isn't fatal, for the Lord holds them with his hand. I have been young and now I am old. And in all my years I have never seen the Lord forsake a man who loves him; nor have I seen the children of the godly go hungry (Psalm 37:23-25 TLB).

Principle

Experience is a strenuous teacher—no graduates, no degrees, some survivors. It enables you to recognize a mistake when you make it again.

Proverb

He who wants the fruit must climb the tree.

Promise

Behold I am coming soon. My reward is with me, and I will give to everyone according to what he has done (Revelation 22:12 NIV).

Principle

The three great essentials to achieve anything worthwhile are first, hard work; second, stick-to-itiveness; third, common sense—Edison.

Proverb

He who eats 'til he is sick must fast 'til he
is well.

Promise

When dining with a rich man, be on your
guard and don't stuff yourself, though it all
tastes so good; for he is trying to bribe
you, and no good is going to come of his
invitation (Proverbs 23:1-3 TLB).

Principle

Many people who go to a physician have no
organic disease, but are merely suffering
from a lack of discretion.

Proverb

He who tells a secret is another man's
servant.

Promise

A gossip betrays a confidence, but a
trustworthy man keeps a secret (Proverbs
11:13 NIV).

Principle

If you think a woman can't keep a secret,
ask one her age or her weight! Men don't
usually give secrets away. They trade them.

Proverb

He who is angry is seldom at ease.

Promise

A wise man restrains his anger and over-looks insults. This is to his credit (Proverbs 19:11 TLB).

Principle

The greatest remedy for anger is delay. For every minute you are angry you lose 60 seconds of happiness.

Proverb

He who plants roses will not reap thistles.

Promise

Do not be deceived: God cannot be mocked.
A man reaps what he sows (Galatians 6:7
NIV).

Principle

Let us endeavor to so live that when we
come to die even the undertaker will be
sorry—Mark Twain.

Proverb

He who nothing questions, nothing learns.

Promise

Determination to be wise is the first step toward becoming wise! And with your wisdom, develop common sense and good judgment (Proverbs 4:7 TLB).

Principle

Don't be afraid to ask dumb questions. They're easier to handle than dumb mistakes.

Proverb

He who gets up one more time than he falls
down will succeed.

Promise

Work hard so God can say to you, "Well
done." Be a good workman, one who does
not need to be ashamed when God exam-
ines your work. Know what his Word says
and means (2 Timothy 2:15 TLB).

Principle

People who succeed face up to a no-win
situation—and win anyway. Even though
they make more mistakes than anyone else,
they are determined to come out on top.

Proverb

He who controls his youth will enjoy his old age.

Promise

Don't let the excitement of being young cause you to forget about your Creator. Honor him in your youth before the evil years come—when you'll no longer enjoy living (Ecclesiastes 12:1 TLB).

Principle

Reputation is something to live up to in your youth and to live down in your old age. A misspent youth may result in a tragic old age.

Proverb

He who fears God has nothing else to fear.

Promise

Don't envy evil men but continue to
reverence the Lord all the time, for surely
you have a wonderful future ahead of you.
There is hope for you yet! (Proverbs
23:17,18 TLB).

Principle

In God I put my trust,
I neither doubt nor fear;
For man can never harm me
With God my Helper near.

Proverb

He who sides with God always wins; to
Him no cause is lost.

Promise

How we thank God for all of this! It is he
who makes us victorious through Jesus
Christ our Lord! If God is on our side, who
can ever be against us? (1 Corinthians 15:57;
Romans 8:31b TLB).

Principle

My great concern is not whether God is on
our side; my great concern is to be on God's
side—Abraham Lincoln.

Proverb

He who stands for nothing is apt to fall for
anything.

Promise

Put on all of God's armor so that you will
be able to stand safe against all strategies
and tricks of Satan (Ephesians 6:11 TLB).

Principle

Stand firm for what you know is right,
It's wise as I have found.
The mighty oak was once a nut
That simply held its ground.

Proverb

He who is in the most trouble usually has
been busy making it.

Promise

I want you to trust me in your times of
trouble, so I can rescue you, and you can
give me glory (Psalm 50:15 TLB).

Principle

If you could kick the person responsible for
most of your troubles, you wouldn't be able
to sit down for six months.

Proverb

He who is born of God should grow to
resemble his Father.

Promise

But grow in spiritual strength and become
better acquainted with our Lord and Savior
Jesus Christ. To him be all glory and
splendid honor, both now and forevermore
(2 Peter 3:18 TLB).

Principle

Some Christians can't be called "pilgrims"
because they don't make any progress. The
knowledge, understanding, and appropria-
tion of God's Word are the means by which
Christians grow to be like the Father.

Proverb

He who spreads the sails of prayer will eventually fly the flag of praise.

Promise

Ask, and you will be given what you ask for. Seek, and you will find. Knock, and the door will be opened (Matthew 7:7 TLB).

Principle

The one concern of the devil is to keep Christians from praying. He fears nothing from prayerless studies, prayerless work, and prayerless religion. He laughs at our toil, mocks at our wisdom, but trembles when we pray—Samuel Chadwick.

Proverb

He who kills time injures eternity.

Promise

Wear shoes that are able to speed you on as you preach the Good News of peace with God. In every battle you will need faith as your shield to stop the fiery arrows aimed at you by Satan (Ephesians 6:15,16 TLB).

Principle

Time is a versatile performer. It flies, marches on, heals all wounds, runs out, will tell, and waits for no man.

Proverb

He who can step on your toes without
messing up your shine is a tactful leader.

Promise

If you want favor with both God and man,
and a reputation for good judgment and
common sense, then trust the Lord com-
pletely; don't ever trust yourself (Proverbs
3:4,5 TLB).

Principle

A wise man is like a pin. His head keeps
him from going too far or saying too much.

Proverb

He who hesitates is not only lost but miles
from the next exit.

Promise

Give glory to the Lord your God before it is
too late, before he causes deep, impene-
trable darkness to fall upon you so that you
stumble and fall upon the dark mountains;
then, when you look for light, you will find
only terrible darkness (Jeremiah 13:16 TLB).

Principle

Delays can be dangerous. He who hesitates
is honked at. He who hesitates is rear-
ended.

Proverb

He who sits in "Z" row may find the
sermon cold.

Promise

Come here and listen to me! I'll pour out
the spirit of wisdom upon you, and make
you wise (Proverbs 1:23 TLB).

Principle

Church members who need defrosting
should be fired up by a few "red-hot"
sermons.

Proverb

He who is walking on clouds is apt to be
carried away.

Promise

Young man, obey your father and your
mother. . . . Take to heart all of their advice.
Every day and all night long their counsel
will lead you and save you from harm;
when you wake up in the morning, let their
instructions guide you into the new day
(Proverbs 6:20-22 TLB).

Principle

Take the world as it is, not as it should be.
To be happy we must face reality.

Proverb

He who accepts evil without protesting against it, is really cooperating with it.

Promise

So give yourselves humbly to God. Resist the devil and he will flee from you (James 4:7 TLB).

Principle

There's nothing consistent about human behavior except its tendency to drift toward evil. The chief evil of many people is not so much in doing evil, but in permitting it.

Proverb

He who sins and repents commends himself
to God.

Promise

Then if my people will humble themselves
and pray, and search for me, and turn from
their wicked ways, I will hear them from
heaven and forgive their sins and heal their
land (2 Chronicles 7:14 TLB).

Principle

To grieve over sin is one thing; to repent is
another. It takes more courage to repent
than to keep on sinning.

Proverb

He who gets his barber's license wants to
get ahead.

Promise

I want to suggest that you finish what you
started to do a year ago, for you were not
only the first to propose this idea, but the
first to begin doing something about it (2
Corinthians 8:10 TLB).

Principle

Even a mule does not get ahead while he's
kicking; neither does a man.

Proverb

He who procrastinates struggles with failure
and lack of fulfillment.

Promise

A wise man thinks ahead; a fool doesn't,
and even brags about it! (Proverbs 13:16
TLB).

Principle

Don't put off until tomorrow what you can
do today; by tomorrow there may be a law
against it.

Proverb

He who is carried away by his own importance seldom has far to walk back.

Promise

It is better to get your hands dirty—and eat,
than to be too proud to work—and starve
(Proverbs 12:9 TLB).

Principle

Success that goes to a man's head usually
pays a very short visit.

Proverb

He who sees an enemy behind every tree is a pessimist.

Promise

The wicked flee when no one is chasing them! But the godly are bold as lions! (Proverbs 28:1 TLB).

Principle

When confronted with a Goliath-size problem which way do you respond: "He's too big to hit," or, like David, "He's too big to miss"?

Proverb

He who shoots often will eventually hit the mark.

Promise

So, my dear brothers, since future victory is sure, be strong and steady, always abounding in the Lord's work, for you know that nothing you do for the Lord is ever wasted as it would be if there were no resurrection (1 Corinthians 15:58 TLB).

Principle

There are four steps to accomplishment: Plan purposefully. Prepare prayerfully. Proceed positively. Pursue persistently. Failure is the path of least persistence.

Proverb

He who has made a mistake and does not
correct it is committing a second mistake.

Promise

A man who refuses to admit his mistakes
can never be successful. But if he confesses
and forsakes them, he gets another chance
(Proverbs 28:13 TLB).

Principle

The only complete mistake is the mistake
from which we learn nothing.

Proverb

He who sees the invisible, hears the
inaudible, and believes the incredible can do
the impossible.

Promise

All that's required is that you really believe
and have no doubt! Listen to me! You can
pray for anything, and if you believe, you
have it; it's yours! (Mark 11:23,24 TLB).

Principle

It's impossible for faith to overdraw its
account on the bank of heaven.

Proverb

He who wipes the child's nose kisses the
mother's cheek.

Promise

We try to live in such a way that no one
will ever be offended or kept back from
finding the Lord by the way we act, so that
no one can find fault with us and blame it
on the Lord (2 Corinthians 6:3 TLB).

Principle

Tact is the ability to put your best foot
forward without stepping on anyone's toes.

Proverb

He who enters the bar very optimistically
often comes out very mist-optically.

Promise

Don't let the sparkle and the smooth taste of
strong wine deceive you. You will see
hallucinations and have delirium tremens,
and you will say foolish, silly things that
would embarrass you no end when sober
(Proverbs 23:31,33 TLB).

Principle

They drink to one another's health,
And yet before they've finished
Their round of toasts, their state of health
Has noticeably diminished.

Proverb

He who has burned his mouth blows on his soup.

Promise

Be careful—watch out for attacks from Satan, your great enemy. He prowls around like a hungry, roaring lion, looking for some victim to tear apart (1 Peter 5:8 TLB).

Principle

A man never knows how careful he can be until he buys a new car or wears white shoes.

Proverb

He who attends church every week avoids
the Easter rush.

Promise

Let us not neglect our church meetings, as
some people do, but encourage and warn
each other, especially now that the day of
his coming back again is drawing near
(Hebrews 10:25 TLB).

Principle

An empty tomb proves Christianity; an
empty church denies it.

Proverb

He who will not learn from anyone except himself has a fool for a teacher.

Promise

A wise man is hungry for truth, while the mocker feeds on trash (Proverbs 15:14 TLB).

Principle

To be humble to superiors is duty; to equals, courtesy; to inferiors, nobility.

Proverb

He who worries interferes with God's
master plan.

Promise

Don't worry about anything; instead, pray
about everything; tell God your needs and
don't forget to thank him for his answers
(Philippians 4:6 TLB).

Principle

Blessed is the man who is too busy to worry
in the daytime, and too sleepy to worry at
night.

Proverb

He who sings his own praises may have the
right tune but the wrong words.

Promise

Proud men end in shame, but the meek
become wise (Proverbs 11:2 TLB).

Principle

The world's most conceited man is the one
who celebrates his birthday by sending his
mother a telegram of congratulations.

Proverb

He who throws dirt may hit his mark but will have dirty hands.

Promise

Your own soul is nourished when you are kind; it is destroyed when you are cruel (Proverbs 14:17 TLB).

Principle

Money will buy a fine dog, but only kindness makes him wag his tail. Be kind to everybody. You never know who might show up on the jury at your trial.

Proverb

He who carries a tale makes a monkey of himself.

Promise

A gossip goes around spreading rumors, while a trustworthy man tries to quiet them (Proverbs 11:13 TLB).

Principle

Those who gossip usually wind up in their own mouth traps. The best way to save face is to keep the lower part shut.

Proverb

He who rides a rocking horse makes motion but no progress.

Promise

Because the Lord God helps me, I will not be dismayed; therefore, I have set my face like flint to do his will, and I know that I will triumph (Isaiah 50:7 TLB).

Principle

You can't go forward or make progress by looking in the rearview mirror.

Proverb

Sometimes he who thinks he's in the groove
is only in the rut.

Promise

Do you not know that the wicked will not
inherit the kingdom of God? Do not be
deceived: Neither the sexually immoral nor
idolaters nor adulterers nor male prostitutes
nor homosexual offenders nor thieves nor
the greedy nor drunkards nor slanderers nor
swindlers will inherit the kingdom of God (1
Corinthians 6:9,10 NIV).

Principle

Oh, what a tangled web we weave, when
first we practice to deceive—Scott.

Proverb

He who gets something for nothing often gripes about its quality.

Promise

But godliness with contentment is great gain. And having food and raiment let us be therewith content (1 Timothy 6:6,8 KJV).

Principle

"Whines" are the products of sour grapes.

Proverb

He who says nothing shows a fine command
of language.

Promise

Keep your mouth closed and you'll stay out
of trouble. A rebel shouts in anger; a wise
man holds his temper in and cools it
(Proverbs 21:23; 29:11 TLB).

Principle

It doesn't do to do much talking when
   you're mad enough to choke,
For the word that hits the hardest is the one
   that's never spoke.
Let the other fellow do the talking till the
   storm has rolled away,
Then he'll do a heap of thinking 'bout the
   things you didn't say.

Proverb

He who deals with the devil will make very small profits.

Promise

For you are the children of your father the devil and you love to do the evil things he does. He was a murderer from the beginning and a hater of truth—there is not an iota of truth in him. When he lies, it is perfectly normal; for he is the father of lies (John 8:44 TLB).

Principle

If you are a child of God and you marry a child of the devil, you will be sure to have constant trouble with your father-in-law.

Proverb

He who is always watching the clock never becomes the man of the hour.

Promise

Read the history books and see—for we were born but yesterday and know so little; our days here on earth are as transient as shadows. But the wisdom of the past will teach you. The experience of others will speak to you (Job 8:8-10 TLB).

Principle

No matter how hard you try to improve on Mother Nature, you're not kidding Father Time. What Mother Nature giveth, Father Time taketh away.

Proverb

He who stays in the valley will never get over the hill.

Promise

This should be your ambition: to live a quiet life, minding your own business and doing your own work, just as we told you before (1 Thessalonians 4:11 TLB).

Principle

Ambition never gets you anywhere until it forms a partnership with blood, sweat, toil, and tears.

Proverb

He who speaks the truth is always at ease.

Promise

A good man's mind is filled with honest
thoughts; an evil man's mind is crammed
with lies (Proverbs 12:5 TLB).

Principle

A good thing about telling the truth is that
you don't have to remember what you said.

Proverb

He who loses his temper should not look for
it.

Promise

A short-tempered man is a fool. He hates
the man who is patient (Proverbs 14:17
TLB).

Principle

Nothing will cook your goose faster than a
boiling-hot temper.

Proverb

He who wants to score must first have a goal.

Promise

So I run straight to the goal with purpose in every step. I fight to win. I'm not just shadow-boxing or playing around (1 Corinthians 9:26 TLB).

Principle

It's more important to know where you're going than to see how fast you can get there.

Proverb

He who is continually finding fault seldom
finds anything else.

Promise

Don't criticize, and then you won't be criti-
cized. For others will treat you as you treat
them (Matthew 7:1,2 TLB).

Principle

Be patient with the faults of others; they
may have to be patient with yours.

Proverb

He who cannot remember the past is
condemned to repeat it.

Promise

Read the history books and see—for we
were born but yesterday and know so little;
our days here on earth are as transient as
shadows. But the wisdom of the past will
teach you (Job 8:8-10 TLB).

Principle

Why is it that nobody listens when history
repeats itself? Every time it does, the price
doubles.

Proverb

He who wears out his pants before his
shoes makes too many contacts in the
wrong places.

Promise

A lazy fellow has trouble all through life;
the good man's path is easy! (Proverbs 15:19
TLB).

Principle

It doesn't do any good to sit up and take
notice if you keep on sitting.

Proverb

He who seeks a quarrel finds it near at hand.

Promise

It is honor for a man to stay out of a fight. Only fools insist on quarreling. It is hard to stop a quarrel once it starts, so don't let it begin (Proverbs 20:3; 17:14 TLB).

Principle

Perhaps the only way to avoid quarreling with your wife is to let her go her way and you go hers.

Proverb

He who is looking for opportunities will find them dressed in work clothes.

Promise

I will be staying here at Ephesus until the holiday of Pentecost, for there is a wide open door for me to preach and teach here. So much is happening, but there are many enemies (1 Corinthians 16:8,9 TLB).

Principle

The trouble with opportunities is that they're always more recognizable going than coming.

Proverb

He who wants to lose a troublesome visitor
should lend him money.

Promise

The rich rule over the poor, and the
borrower is servant to the lender. (Proverbs
22:7 NIV).

Principle

Money separates more friends than it unites.
It not only changes hands—it changes
people.

Proverb

He who knows little too often shares it.

Promise

Yes, if you want better insight and discernment, and are searching for them as you would for lost money or hidden treasure, then wisdom will be given you, and knowledge of God himself; you will soon learn the importance of reverence for the Lord and of trusting him (Proverbs 2:3-5 TLB).

Principle

No one gives advice with more enthusiasm than an ignorant person. If you think education is costly, try ignorance.

Proverb

He who looks for trouble does not need a search warrant.

Promise

Yet man is born to trouble as surely as sparks fly upward (Job 5:7 NIV).

Principle

A lot of trouble is caused by our yearnings getting ahead of our earnings.

Proverb

He who laughs, lasts.

Promise

A happy face means a glad heart; a sad face means a breaking heart (Proverbs 15:13 TLB).

Principle

A good laugh is the best medicine, whether you are sick or not. Fortune smiles on the man who can laugh at himself.

Proverb

He who has learned to obey will know how
to command.

Promise

God blesses those who obey him; happy the
man who puts his trust in the Lord
(Proverbs 16:20 TLB).

Principle

Every great person first learned how to
obey, whom to obey, and when to obey.

Proverb

He who falls in love with himself will have
no competition.

Promise

Do nothing out of selfish ambition or vain
conceit, but in humility consider others
better than yourselves. Each of you should
look not only to your own interests, but also
to the interest of others (Philippians 2:3,4
NIV).

Principle

Those who believe only in themselves live
in a very small world.

Proverb

He who is cheated twice by the same man
is an accomplice with the cheater.

Promise

Some men enjoy cheating, but the cake they
buy with such ill-gotten gains will turn to
gravel in their mouths. The Lord despises
every kind of cheating (Proverbs 20:17,10
TLB).

Principle

Live your life so that your autograph will be
wanted instead of your fingerprints.

Proverb

He who smells flowers and looks around for a coffin is a cynic.

Promise

Men scoff at me and say, "What is this word of the Lord you keep talking about? If these threats of yours are really from God, why don't they come true?" (Jeremiah 17:15 TLB).

Principle

A cynic is a man who knows the price of everything, and the value of nothing—Oscar Wilde. He looks both ways before crossing a one-way street.

Proverb

He who isn't himself on Sundays is a hypocrite.

Promise

That man should not think he will receive anything from the Lord; he is a double-minded man, unstable in all he does (James 1:7,8 NIV).

Principle

The hypocrite believes that life is what you fake it.

Proverb

He who is kind to his wife is kind to
himself.

Promise

Husbands, love your wives, just as Christ
loved the church and gave himself up for
her (Ephesians 5:25 NIV).

Principle

"Help your wife," a home economics
lecturer advised. "When she washes the
dishes, wash the dishes with her; when she
mops the floor, mop the floor with her."

Proverb

He who thinks before he speaks is silent
most of the time.

Promise

Even a fool is thought to be wise when he is
silent. It pays him to keep his mouth shut
(Proverbs 17:28 TLB).

Principle

Silence is evidence of a superb command of
the English language.

Proverb

He who has made a start has half the job done.

Promise

Do you see a man skilled in his work? He will serve before kings; he will not serve before obscure men (Proverbs 22:29 NIV).

Principle

The more push a person possesses, the less pull he needs. Every great man of God has been a self-starter.

Proverb

He who beefs too much may find himself in
stew.

Promise

I said to myself, I'm going to quit complaining! I'll keep quiet, especially when the
ungodly are around me (Psalm 39:1 TLB).

Principle

Those individuals who always are quick
With specific complaints that they're citing
Will back off immediately when they are
  asked
To please submit them in writing—Erica H.
  Stux.

Proverb

He who pours water hastily into a bottle
spills more than he saves.

Promise

So be careful how you act; these are
difficult days. Don't be fools; be wise: make
the most of every opportunity you have for
doing good. Don't act thoughtlessly, but try
to find out and do whatever the Lord wants
you to (Ephesians 5:15-17 TLB).

Principle

Great haste makes great waste—Franklin.
Make haste slowly—Caesar. Though I am
always in haste, I'm never in a hurry—
Wesley.

Proverb

He who makes no mistakes does not usually make anything.

Promise

Love forgets mistakes; nagging about them parts the best of friends (Proverbs 17:9 TLB).

Principle

The man who never makes mistakes loses many chances to learn something.

Proverb

He who leaves home to set the world on fire often comes back for more matches.

Promise

Teach a wise man, and he will be the wiser; teach a good man, and he will learn more. Get all the advice you can and be wise the rest of your life (Proverbs 9:9; 19:20 TLB).

Principle

Experience is the thing you have left when everything else is gone. It's one thing you can't get for nothing.

Proverb

He who longs to sing will always find a
song.

Promise

And let us not get tired of doing what is
right, for after a while we reap a harvest of
blessing if we don't get discouraged and
give up (Galatians 6:9 TLB).

Principle

Most men fail, not through lack of education, but from lack of dogged determination,
from lack of dauntless will.

Proverb

He who brings sunshine into the lives of others cannot keep it from himself.

Promise

But happy is the man who has the God of Jacob as his helper, whose hope is in the Lord his God—the God who made both earth and heaven, the seas and everything in them (Psalm 146:5,6 TLB).

Principle

Laughter is the sun that drives winter from the human face—Victor Hugo. A laugh is worth a hundred groans in any market.

Proverb

He who thinks he's a wit is usually only
half right.

Promise

Wisdom shouts in the streets for a hearing.
She calls out to the crowds along Main
Street, and to the judges in their courts, and
to everyone in all the land: "You simple-
tons!" she cries. "How long will you go on
being fools? How long will you scoff at
wisdom and fight the facts?" (Proverbs
1:20-22 TLB).

Principle

A fool attempting to be witty is an object of
profoundest pity.

Proverb

He who lives it up may have to live it down.

Promise

The man who sets a trap for others will get caught in it himself. Roll a boulder on someone, and it will roll back and crush you (Proverbs 26:27 TLB).

Principle

Logical consequences are the scarecrows of fools and the beacons of wise men—Thomas Huxley.

Proverb

He who wants to soar with the eagles must
avoid running with turkeys.

Promise

But they that wait upon the Lord shall
renew their strength; they shall mount up
with wings as eagles; they shall run, and not
be weary; and they shall walk, and not faint
(Isaiah 40:31 KJV).

Principle

Tell me thy company, and I will tell thee
what thou art—Cervantes. It is better to be
alone than in bad company—Washington.

Proverb

He who has four but spends five has no
need of a purse.

Promise

Don't weary yourself trying to get rich.
Why waste your time? For riches can
disappear as though they had the wings of a
bird! (Proverbs 23:4,5 TLB).

Principle

The trouble with some families is that
they have Cadillac tastes and compact
incomes. Families that buy together often
cry together.

Proverb

He who works in summer's heat will not
hunger in winter's frost.

Promise

He who gathers crops in summer is a wise
son, but he who sleeps during harvest is a
disgraceful son (Proverbs 10:5 NIV).

Principle

Work for the Lord. The pay isn't much, but
the retirement plan is out of this world.

Proverb

He who flees temptation should not leave a forwarding address.

Promise

Happy is the man who doesn't give in and do wrong when he is tempted, for afterwards he will get as his reward the crown of life that God has promised those who love him (James 1:12 TLB).

Principle

Opportunity knocks only once; temptation leans on the doorbell.

Proverb

He who runs into debt usually has to crawl out.

Promise

Owe no man any thing, but to love one another: for he that loveth another hath fulfilled the law (Romans 13:8 KJV).

Principle

The world's greatest humorist is probably the man who named them "easy payments." Debt and misery live on the same street.

Proverb

He who is doing nothing is seldom without helpers.

Promise

A lazy fellow is a pain to his employers—like smoke in their eyes or vinegar that sets the teeth on edge (Proverbs 10:26 TLB).

Principle

Sign on minister's desk: "If you have nothing to do, please don't do it here."

Proverb

He who speaks with a forked tongue is
probably a snake in the grass.

Promise

He who guards his lips guards his soul, but
he who speaks rashly will come to ruin.
Some people like to make cutting remarks,
but the words of the wise soothe and heal
(Proverbs 13:3 NIV; 12:18 TLB).

Principle

Medical doctors measure physical health by
how the tongue looks. The Great Physician
measures spiritual health by how the tongue
acts. The most untamable thing in the world
has its den just behind the teeth.

Proverb

He who doesn't know where he's going will probably end up someplace else.

Promise

You are my hiding place from every storm of life; you even keep me from getting into trouble! You surround me with songs of victory. I will instruct you (says the Lord) and guide you along the best pathway for your life; I will advise you and watch your progress (Psalm 32:7,8 TLB).

Principle

Keep your head and your heart going in the right direction and you'll not have to worry about your feet.

Proverb

He who walks in when others walk out is a true friend.

Promise

There are "friends" who pretend to be friends, but there is a friend who sticks closer than a brother (Proverbs 18:24 TLB).

Principle

A real friend is one who will tell you of your faults and follies in prosperity, and assist you with his hand and heart in adversity.

Proverb

He who wants his dreams to come true
must stay awake.

Promise

Do not love sleep or you will grow poor;
stay awake and you will have food to spare
(Proverbs 20:13 NIV).

Principle

No dream comes true until you wake up
and go to work. Between tomorrow's
dream and yesterday's regret is today's
opportunity.

Proverb

He who wants to catch trout should not fish in a herring barrel.

Promise

The way of a fool seems right to him, but a wise man listens to advice (Proverbs 12:15 NIV).

Principle

Knowledge can be memorized. Wisdom must think things through. The man who knows *how* will always find a place in life, but the man who knows *why* will likely be his boss.

Proverb

He who hunts two hares leaves one and
loses the other.

Promise

Come near to God and he will come near to
you. Wash your hands, you sinners, and
purify your hearts, you double-minded
(James 4:8 NIV).

Principle

The man who seeks one thing in life, and
but one, may hope to achieve it before life
is done; but he who seeks all things,
wherever he goes, only reaps from the
hopes which around him he sows, a harvest
of barren results.

Proverb

He who lives without self-control is exposed
to grievous ruin.

Promise

Like a city whose walls are broken down is
a man who lacks self-control (Proverbs
25:28 NIV).

Principle

The best time to keep your shirt on is when
you're hot under the collar.

Proverb

He who has time to burn will never give the world much light.

Promise

Teach us to number our days aright, that we may gain a heart of wisdom (Psalm 90:12 NIV).

Principle

Few things are more dangerous to a person's character than having nothing to do and plenty of time in which to do it. Killing time is not murder, it's suicide.

Proverb

He who is a man of silence is a man of sense.

Promise

A wise man holds his tongue. Only a fool blurts out everything he knows; that only leads to sorrow and trouble (Proverbs 10:14 TLB).

Principle

You must speak up to be heard, but sometimes you have to shut up to be appreciated. If there's a substitute for brains, it has to be silence.

Proverb

He who loses his head is usually the last
one to miss it.

Promise

It is better to be slow-tempered than
famous; it is better to have self-control than
to control an army (Proverbs 16:32 TLB).

Principle

People who fly into a rage always make a
bad landing. The world needs more warm
hearts and fewer hot heads.

Proverb

He who wants to go to heaven must not neglect flight training.

Promise

So you also must be ready, because the Son of Man will come at an hour when you do not expect him (Matthew 24:44 NIV).

Principle

A lot of people who are worrying about the future ought to be preparing for it. Get ready for eternity—you're going to spend a lot of time there.

Proverb

He who is waiting for something to turn
up might be smart to start with his own
shirt-sleeves.

Promise

He who works his land will have abundant
food, but he who chases fantasies lacks
judgment (Proverbs 12:11 NIV).

Principle

About the only thing that comes to him who
waits is old age. No one can build a
reputation on what he's going to do
tomorrow.

Proverb

He who has an axe to grind often flies off the handle!

Promise

A hot-tempered man stirs up dissension, but a patient man calms a quarrel (Proverbs 15:18 NIV).

Principle

If you speak when you're angry, you'll make the best speech you'll ever regret. Anger is only one letter short of danger.

Proverb

He who sleeps on railroad tracks wakes up
with split personality.

Promise

A man who strays from the path of understanding comes to rest in the company of
the dead (Proverbs 21:16 NIV).

Principle

The foolish and dead alone never change
their opinions—James Lowell.

Proverb

He who digs up facts is getting better exercise than he who jumps to conclusions.

Promise

What a shame—yes, how stupid!—to decide before knowing the facts! Any story sounds true until someone tells the other side and sets the record straight (Proverbs 18:13,17 TLB).

Principle

Those who jump to their own conclusion cannot expect a happy landing.

Proverb

He who writes a book extolling atheism—
and then prays that it will be a bestseller—is
a hypocrite.

Promise

That man is a fool who says to himself,
"There is no God!" Anyone who talks like
that is warped and evil and cannot really be
a good person at all (Psalm 14:1 TLB).

Principle

It must be a problem for two-faced people
to put their best face forward. They never
intend to be what they pretend to be.

Proverb

He who sows wild oats should not pray for a crop failure.

Promise

He who sows wickedness reaps trouble, and the rod of his fury will be destroyed (Proverbs 22:8 NIV).

Principle

The price of wheat, wool, and corn goes up and down, but the price of wild oats stays the same. When a youth begins to sow wild oats, it's time for father to start the threshing machine.

Proverb

He who thinks by the inch and talks by the
yard deserves to be kicked by the foot.

Promise

Don't talk so much. You keep putting your
foot in your mouth. Be sensible and turn off
the flow! When a good man speaks, he is
worth listening to, but the words of fools
are a dime a dozen (Proverbs 10:19,20 TLB).

Principle

Usually the first screw that gets loose in a
person's head is the one that controls the
tongue. The best way to save face is to stop
shooting it off.

Proverb

He who continually watches the clock will always be one of the hands.

Promise

I walked by the field of a certain lazy fellow and saw that it was overgrown with thorns, and covered with weeds; and its walls were broken down. Then, as I looked, I learned this lesson: "A little extra sleep, a little more slumber, a little folding of the hands to rest" means that poverty will break in upon you suddenly like a robber, and violently like a bandit (Proverbs 24:30-34 TLB).

Principle

God gives us the ingredients for our daily bread, but He expects us to do the baking.

Proverb

He who repeats the garbage he hears about another is the real slanderer.

Promise

To hate is to be a liar; to slander is to be a fool. The tongue that brings healing is a tree of life, but a deceitful tongue crushes the spirit (Proverbs 10:18 TLB; 15:4 NIV).

Principle

At the last count, slander was running down more people than automobiles. It's a "negative" that is developed and then enlarged.

Proverb

He who gets to the end of his rope should tie a knot and hang on.

Promise

A man's courage can sustain his broken body, but when courage dies, what hope is left? (Proverbs 18:14 TLB).

Principle

When you get into a tight place and everything goes against you, till it seems as though you could not hold on a minute longer, never give up then, for that is just the place and time that the tide will turn— Harriet Beecher Stowe.

Proverb

He who is not afraid to go out on a limb
will enjoy the fruit.

Promise

You can never please God without faith,
without depending on him. Anyone who
wants to come to God must believe that
there is a God and that he rewards those
who sincerely look for him (Hebrews 11:6
TLB).

Principle

Both faith and fear sail into the harbor of
your mind, but only faith should be allowed
to anchor. Feed your faith and your fears
will starve to death.

Proverb

He who gathers roses must not fear the
thorns.

Promise

To keep me from becoming conceited
because of these surpassingly great revela-
tions, there was given me a thorn in my
flesh, a messenger of Satan, to torment me.
Three times I pleaded with the Lord to take
it away from me. But he said to me, "My
grace is sufficient for you, for my power is
made perfect in weakness" (2 Corinthians
12:7-9a NIV).

Principle

This world that we're a-living in is mighty
hard to beat; you get a thorn with every
rose, but ain't the roses sweet?

Proverb

He who tolerates the devil soon endorses his program.

Promise

Go ahead and prepare for the conflict, but victory comes from God (Proverbs 21:31 TLB). Stand firm when he [Satan] attacks. Trust the Lord; and remember that other Christians all around the world are going through these sufferings too (1 Peter 5:9 TLB).

Principle

The chief evil of many people consists not so much in doing evil, but in permitting it.

Proverb

He who doesn't wait until the rain falls to start building his ark is a wise planner.

Promise

Noah was another who trusted God. When he heard God's warning about the future, Noah believed him even though there was then no sign of a flood, and wasting no time, he built the ark and saved his family. Noah's belief in God was in direct contrast to the sin and disbelief of the rest of the world—which refused to obey—and because of his faith he became one of those God has accepted (Hebrews 11:7 TLB).

Principle

No farmer ever plowed a field by turning it over in his mind.

Proverb

He who does not advance, retreats.

Promise

Be strong and courageous, because you will lead these people to inherit the land I swore to their forefathers to give them. Be strong and very courageous. Be careful to obey all the law my servant Moses gave you; do not turn from it to the right or to the left, that you may be successful wherever you go (Joshua 1:6,7 NIV).

Principle

Progress always involves a certain amount of risk. After all, you can't steal second base with one foot on first.

Proverb

He who spanks his child should have a
definite end in view.

Promise

Don't fail to correct your children; discipline
won't hurt them! They won't die if you use
a stick on them! Punishment will keep them
out of hell (Proverbs 23:13,14 TLB).

Principle

A pat on the back develops character, if it is
administered young enough, often enough,
and low enough.

Proverb

He who growls all day will be dog-tired at night.

Promise

In everything you do, stay away from complaining and arguing, so that no one can speak a word of blame against you (Philippians 2:14,15 TLB).

Principle

Complaining is the thing to try when all else fails. Strong minds suffer without complaining; weak minds complain without suffering.

Proverb

He who buries his head in the sand won't leave any footprints.

Promise

Work hard and become a leader; be lazy and never succeed (Proverbs 12:24 TLB).

Principle

Failure always catches up with those who sit down and wait for success.

Proverb

He who loses his temper usually loses.

Promise

A wise man controls his temper. He knows that anger causes mistakes (Proverbs 14:29 TLB).

Principle

Self-control is giving up smoking cigarettes; extreme self-control is not telling anybody about it.

Proverb

He who says he knows everything sleeps in a fool's hallway.

Promise

I want those already wise to become the wiser and become leaders by exploring the depths of meaning in these nuggets of truth. How does a man become wise? The first step is to trust and reverence the Lord! (Proverbs 1:5-7 TLB).

Principle

Conceit is what makes a foolish little squirt think he's a fountain of knowledge.

Proverb

He who constantly talks about his inferiors
hasn't any.

Promise

Don't criticize and speak evil about each
other, dear brothers. If you do, you will be
fighting against God's law of loving one
another, declaring it is wrong.... So what
right do you have to judge or criticize
others? (James 4:11,12 TLB).

Principle

Handling criticism: If it's untrue, disregard
it; if it's unfair, keep from irritation; if it's
ignorant, smile; if it's justified, learn from it.

Proverb

He who diets goes to great lengths to avoid great widths.

Promise

Listen, my son, and be wise, and keep your heart on the right path. Do not join those who drink too much wine or gorge themselves on meat, for drunkards and gluttons become poor, and drowsiness clothes them in rags (Proverbs 23:19-21 NIV).

Principle

Everybody is so diet-conscious these days that if someone says you're not half the man you used to be, it's considered a compliment. Being on a diet requires great *won't* power.

Proverb

He who thinks it permissible to tell "white
lies" soon grows color-blind.

Promise

Do you want a long, good life? Then watch
your tongue! Keep your lips from lying
(Psalm 34:12,13 TLB).

Principle

Just why do men lie about each other when
the plain truth would be bad enough?

Proverb

He who weaves through traffic may wind
up in stitches.

Promise

The path of the godly leads away from evil;
he who follows that path is safe. Before
every man there lies a wide and pleasant
road he thinks is right, but it ends in death
(Proverbs 16:17,25 TLB).

Principle

Always try to drive so that your license will
expire before you do. Drive carefully, and
don't insist on your rites.

Proverb

He who wants to finish the race must stay
on the track.

Promise

Since we have such a huge crowd of men of
faith watching us from the grandstands, let
us strip off anything that slows us down or
holds us back, and especially those sins that
wrap themselves so tightly around our feet
and trip us up; and let us run with patience
the particular race that God has set before
us (Hebrews 12:1 TLB).

Principle

In golf and in life, it's the follow through
that makes the difference.

Proverb

He who has nothing to do is quickly tired of his own company.

Promise

Hard work means prosperity; only a fool idles away his time (Proverbs 12:11 TLB).

Principle

Counting time is not as important as making time count—Walker.

Proverb

He who gets on a high horse is riding for a fall.

Promise

There is one thing worse than a fool, and that is a man who is conceited (Proverbs 26:12 TLB).

Principle

A sure cure for conceit is a visit to the cemetery, where eggheads and boneheads get equal billing.

Proverb

He who has an inflated opinion of himself is
likely a poor judge of human nature.

Promise

Pride goes before destruction and haughti-
ness before a fall. Better poor and humble
than proud and rich. He who humbles
himself shall be honored (Proverbs 16:18,19;
Luke 14:11b TLB).

Principle

When you know you've got humility, you've
lost it! Humility is to make a right estimate
of one's self—Spurgeon.

Proverb

He who has no life strategy does not know why he is doing what he is doing.

Promise

We should make plans—counting on God to direct us. In everything you do, put God first, and he will direct you and crown your efforts with success (Proverbs 16:9; 3:6 TLB).

Principle

It is better to say, "This one thing I do," than to say, "These 40 things I dabble in." The secret of success is constancy of purpose—Disraeli.

Proverb

He who prays when the sun is shining will know how to pray when the storm hits.

Promise

Seek the Lord while you can find him. Call upon him now while he is near (Isaiah 55:6 TLB). Those who search for me shall surely find me (Proverbs 8:17b TLB).

Principle

Sign outside a Dallas church: "Last chance to pray before entering freeway." Prayer is the stop that keeps you going.

Proverb

He who is willing to face the music will someday lead the band.

Promise

Anyone willing to be corrected is on the pathway to life. Anyone refusing has lost his chance (Proverbs 10:17 TLB).

Principle

The triumphal song of life would lose its melody without its minor keys. The address of character is often carved on the corner of Adversity Avenue and Determination Drive.

Proverb

He who loses his head probably doesn't miss it.

Promise

Wine gives false courage; hard liquor leads to brawls; what fools men are to let it master them, making them reel drunkenly down the street! (Proverbs 20:1 TLB).

Principle

A "hangover" is something that occupies the head you neglected to use last night.

Proverb

He who forgets the language of thanksgiving
will never be on speaking terms with real
happiness.

Promise

Pray all the time. Ask God for anything in
line with the Holy Spirit's wishes. Plead
with him, reminding him of your needs, and
keep praying earnestly for all Christians
everywhere (Ephesians 6:18 TLB).

Principle

There's always something to be thankful for.
If you can't pay your bills, you can be
thankful you're not one of your creditors.

Proverb

He who eats forbidden fruit will end up in bad jam.

Promise

Different kinds of fruit trees can quickly be identified by examining their fruit. So the trees having the inedible fruit are chopped down and thrown on the fire. Yes, the way to identify a tree or a person is by the kind of fruit produced (Matthew 7:17,19,20 TLB).

Principle

Results are what you expect and consequences are what you get.

Proverb

He who goes to see a psychiatrist should
have his head examined.

Promise

Open the gates that the righteous nation
may enter, the nation that keeps faith. You
will keep in perfect peace him whose mind
is steadfast, because he trusts in you (Isaiah
26:2,3 NIV).

Principle

Practicing psychiatry without faith in God is
like meeting a hungry man and giving him a
toothpick.

Proverb

He who wants to avoid traffic congestion
should travel the straight and narrow road.

Promise

Enter through the narrow gate. For wide is
the gate and broad is the road that leads to
destruction, and many enter through it
(Matthew 7:13 NIV).

Principle

Maybe the reason we have traffic problems
is because the traffic has become as dense
as the drivers.

Proverb

He who crosses ocean twice without taking bath is dirty double-crosser.

Promise

Lord! Help! Godly men are fast disappearing. Where in all the world can dependable men be found? Everyone deceives and flatters and lies. There is no sincerity left (Psalm 12:1,2 TLB).

Principle

The wolf in sheep's clothing is a fitting emblem of a hypocrite. Every virtuous man would rather meet an open foe than a pretended friend who is a traitor at heart.

Proverb

He who blows out the other fellow's candle won't make his own shine any brighter.

Promise

For though once your heart was full of darkness, now it is full of light from the Lord, and your behavior should show it! Because of this light within you, you should do only what is good and right and true (Ephesians 5:8,9 TLB).

Principle

You'll never move up if you're continually running somebody down. Two things are hard on the heart: running up stairs and running down people.

Proverb

He who does not find time for exercise may
have to find time for illness.

Promise

For physical training is of some value, but
godliness has value for all things, holding
promise for both the present life and the life
to come (1 Timothy 4:8 NIV).

Principle

Too many people confine their exercise to
jumping to conclusions, running up bills,
stretching the truth, bending over backward,
lying down on the job, sidestepping respon-
sibility, and pushing their luck.

Proverb

He who swims in sin will sink in shame.

Promise

He who leads the upright along an evil path will fall into his own trap, but the blameless will receive a good inheritance (Proverbs 28:10 NIV).

Principle

Shame is the stirring of conscience after the act—Maria Edgeworth. Shame can be good for you. It may lead to decency—Ben Hecht.

Proverb

He who is his own lawyer has a fool for a client.

Promise

A man is a fool to trust himself! But those who use God's wisdom are safe (Proverbs 28:26 TLB).

Principle

Trust in yourself, and you are doomed to disappointment. Trust in your friends, and they will die and leave you. Trust in your money, and you may have it taken from you. Trust in reputation, and some slanderous tongue will slash it. Trust in God, and you will never be confounded.

Proverb

He who wants to trick the fox must rise
early.

Promise

Morning by morning, O Lord, you hear my
voice; morning by morning I lay my
requests before you and wait in expectation
(Psalm 5:3 NIV).

Principle

It is the early rising and the well-spending
of the day that is the unbeatable combina-
tion to success.

Proverb

He who keeps his foot on first can't steal
second base.

Promise

Yes, be bold and strong! Banish fear and
doubt! For remember, the Lord your God is
with you wherever you go (Joshua 1:9 TLB).

Principle

It's all right to be cautious—but even a
turtle never gets anywhere until he sticks
his neck out.

Proverb

He who praises himself can drown in a tumblerful of water.

Promise

Don't brag about your plans for tomorrow—wait and see what happens. Don't praise yourself; let others do it! (Proverbs 27:1,2 TLB).

Principle

Remember: When you're praised to the sky, it's best to keep your feet on the ground.

Proverb

He who is always leaning on his family tree
never seems to get out of the woods.

Promise

Happy is the man with a level-headed son;
sad the mother of a rebel. Ill-gotten gain
brings no lasting happiness; right living does
(Proverbs 10:1,2 TLB).

Principle

You can't make a place for yourself under
the sun if you keep sitting in the shade of
the family tree.

Proverb

He who blows his own horn is usually off-key.

Promise

Don't be conceited, sure of your own wisdom. Instead, trust and reverence the Lord, and turn your back on evil; when you do that, then you will be given renewed healthy and vitality (Proverbs 3:7,8 TLB).

Principle

The head never begins to swell until the mind stops growing. It's unfortunate that swelled heads aren't painful.

Proverb

He who cannot forgive others breaks the
bridge over which he himself must pass.

Promise

Your heavenly Father will forgive you if
you forgive those who sin against you
(Matthew 6:14 TLB).

Principle

Doing an injury puts you below your
enemy; revenging a wrong makes you but
even with him; forgiving it sets you above
him.

Proverb

He who kills time buries opportunities.

Promise

And remember why he is waiting. He is
giving us time to get his message of salva-
tion out to others (2 Peter 3:15 TLB).

Principle

The reason most people don't recognize
opportunity is that it's usually going around
disguised as work.

Index